Rocks

Hard, Soft, Smooth, and Rough

Written by Natalie M. Rosinsky
Illustrated by Matthew John

Content Adviser: Dr. Jim Walker, Professor of Geology, Northern Illinois University, DeKalb, Illinois
Reading Adviser: Lauren A. Liang, M.A., Literacy Education, University of Minnesota, Minneapolis, Minnesota

AMAZING SCIENCE

PICTURE WINDOW BOOKS
Minneapolis, Minnesota

Editor: Nadia Higgins
Designer: Melissa Voda
Page production: The Design Lab
The illustrations in this book were prepared digitally.

PICTURE WINDOW BOOKS
151 Good Counsel Drive
P.O. Box 669
Mankato, MN 56002-0669
1-877-845-8392
www.picturewindowbooks.com

Printed in the United States of America.

 All books published by Picture Window Books
are manufactured with paper containing at least
10 percent post-consumer waste.

Library of Congress Cataloging-in-Publication Data
Rosinsky, Natalie M. (Natalie Myra)
  Rocks : hard, soft, smooth, and rough / by Natalie M.
Rosinsky ; illustration by Matthew John.
    v. cm. — (Amazing science) Includes bibliographical
references and index.
  Contents: The story of rocks—Igneous rocks—
Sedimentary rocks—Metamorphic rocks—Activities—Rock
solid facts.
  ISBN-13: 978-1-4048-0015-1 (hardcover)
  ISBN-10: 1-4048-0015-8 (hardcover)
  ISBN-13: 978-1-4048-0334-3 (paperback)
  ISBN-10: 1-4048-0334-3 (paperback)
  1. Rocks—Juvenile literature. [1. Rocks.] I. John,
Matthew, ill. II. Title.
  QE432.2 .R67 2003
  552—dc21   2002005737

TABLE OF CONTENTS

The Story of Rocks

See the rock at your feet? Pick it up.
Hold it in your hands.

Is it smooth and sparkly? Is it soft and sandy? Is it marked with the shape of a shell? Look closely at a rock, and you can learn its story.

Fun fact: Some rocks are four billion years old. (That's 4,000,000,000 years!) Think of all the stories rocks can tell.

A lot of things can happen to rocks. They can crack. They can break into a million tiny pieces. They can be pressed or squeezed together.

Rocks can even melt. Pools of hot, melted rock hide deep inside the earth.

Fun fact: The ground underneath oceans, fields, beaches, and forests is rock.

You might see specks or larger stripes of different colors in your rock. These specks and stripes are different kinds of minerals. Minerals are the basic building blocks of rocks.

Rubies and diamonds are minerals. People carve them into gems that sparkle in necklaces and rings.

ruby

diamond

Fun fact: Diamonds are the hardest natural things in the world. Diamonds are so strong they can even cut through steel.

Igneous Rocks

Rocks form in three ways. In the first way, melted rock bubbles up from inside the earth. Then it cools down and becomes hard igneous rock.

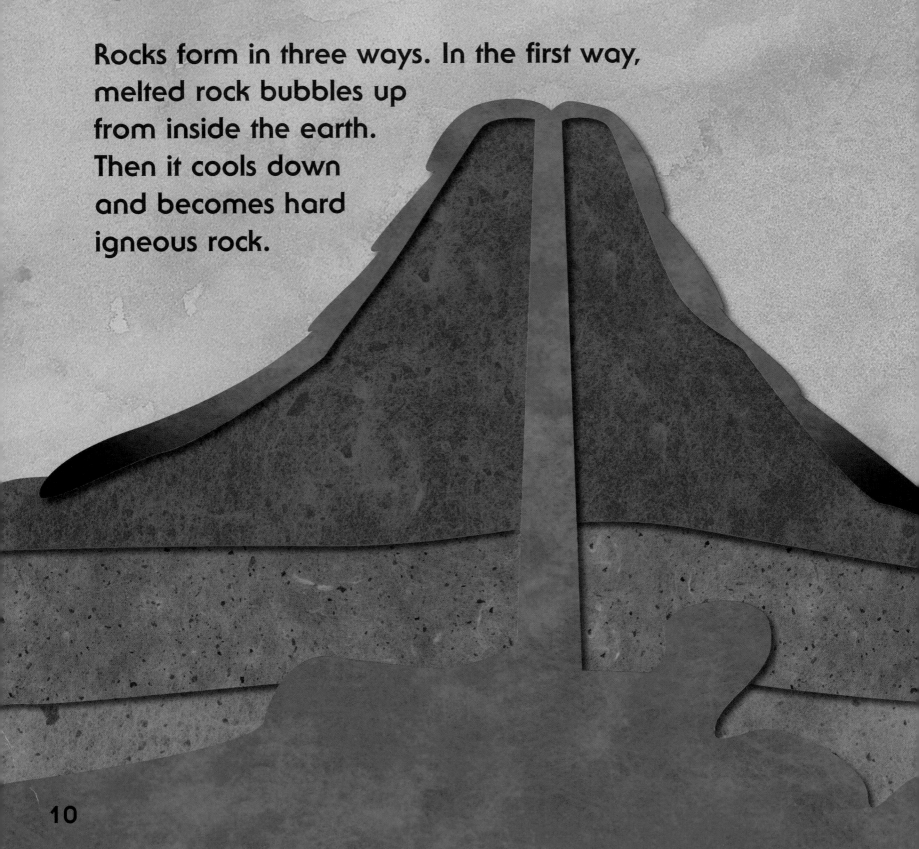

If your rock looks like black glass, it may be obsidian.
Obsidian is an igneous rock that bubbled up from
inside the earth and cooled off above ground. Rough,
freckled granite is an igneous rock that
cooled underground.

obsidian

granite

Fun fact: Native Americans once carved obsidian
into sharp knives and arrowheads. Speckled granite
is often used for gravestones and countertops.

Sedimentary Rocks

Rocks also form when sand and other natural things are squeezed together until they turn hard. This second kind of rock is called sedimentary rock. These rocks are a little softer than igneous rocks.

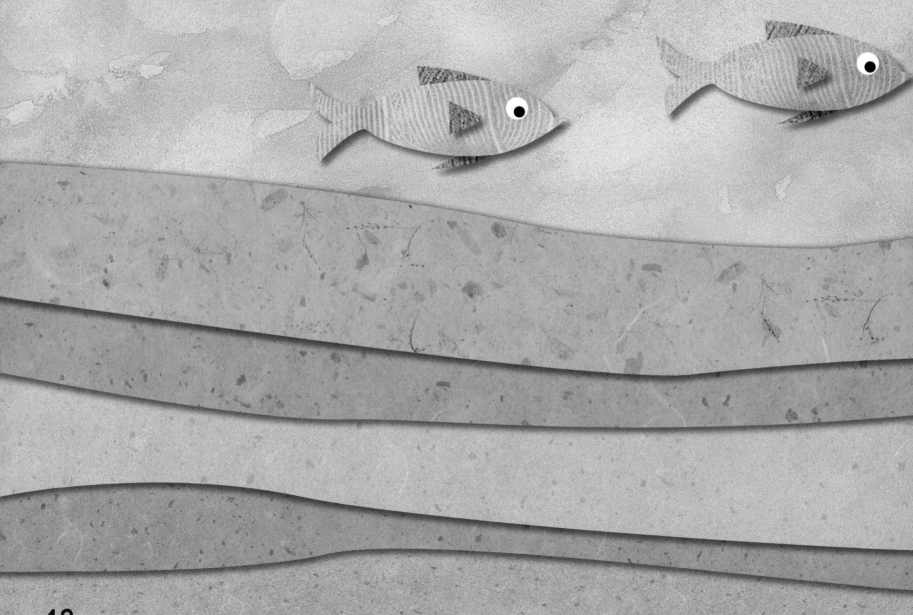

Plants, animal bodies, shells, sand, and chips of other rocks pile up on the bottom of oceans and rivers. This mixture is called sediment. As the mixture piles up, it gets heavy, and the sediment at the bottom gets squeezed together. It turns harder and harder until it is rock—sedimentary rock. This rock can take millions of years to form.

Fun fact: In cliffs and canyons, you can sometimes see different layers of sediment. Some layers are as tall as skyscrapers.

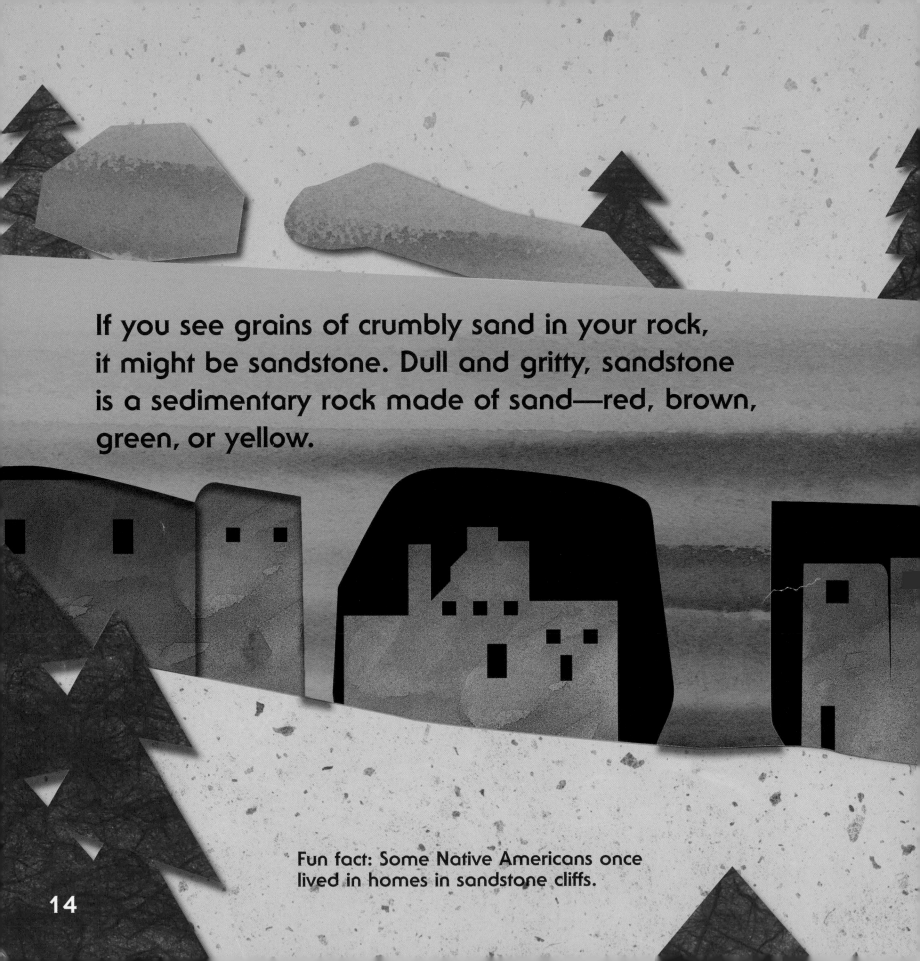

If you see grains of crumbly sand in your rock,
it might be sandstone. Dull and gritty, sandstone
is a sedimentary rock made of sand—red, brown,
green, or yellow.

Fun fact: Some Native Americans once
lived in homes in sandstone cliffs.

If you see squiggles and bumps from little shells and skeletons in your rock, it might be limestone. Limestone, another sedimentary rock, is made of shells from ocean animals that lived a long time ago.

Fun fact: Today, people use limestone to make sidewalks and buildings.

Some sedimentary rocks tell stories about the past—stories of forgotten forests and vanished seas. They tell tales of creatures that swam, slithered, or crept.

Fossils are made from plants and animals that died thousands or millions of years ago. The plants and animals became buried in layers of sediment. Over time, they turned into rock.

Fun fact: Scientists learn about dinosaurs by studying fossils of bones, teeth, eggs, nests, and droppings. Each fossil is a clue. For example, the shape of a dinosaur tooth can show whether a dinosaur ate meat or plants.

Metamorphic Rocks

The third kind of rock is made from other rocks. Heat and pressure deep inside the earth can change rocks from one kind to another. Metamorphic rocks can come from igneous or sedimentary rock. After time, the heat and pressure can even turn a metamorphic rock into a new metamorphic rock.

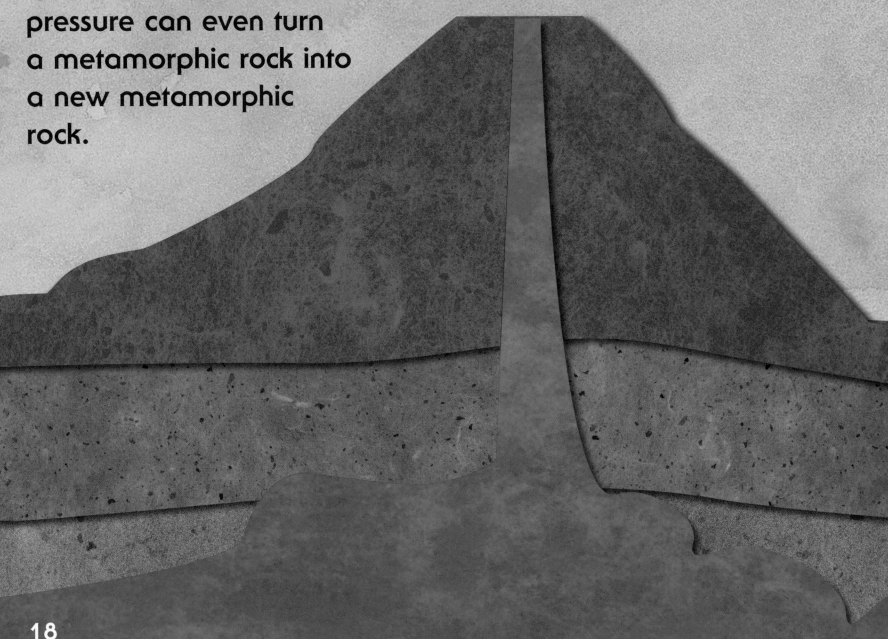

If your rock is hard and full of colorful swirls, it might be marble. Marble is a metamorphic rock made from limestone that cooked inside the earth.

marble

Fun fact: Artists carve marble into statues that tell their own special stories.

Rocks are all around you. Rocks lie at your feet or sit silently by the river's edge. Rocks make a giant cliff, a magnificent building, or a grand sculpture. Rocks hang around your neck or sparkle on your fingers. Look closely at them. What stories do these rocks tell?

20

Rocks Chart

	Kind of Rock	Colors	What It Feels Like	Uses
Obsidian	Igneous	Shiny black	Hard and glassy	Indian arrowheads
Granite	Igneous	A mix of gray, white, pink, or red	Hard and rough	Gravestones, buildings, monuments
Sandstone	Sedimentary	Red, brown, green, or yellow	Grainy and crumbly	Buildings
Limestone	Sedimentary	Tan, gray, or yellow	Can be soft and chalky, or coarse and hard	Buildings, sidewalks
Marble	Metamorphic (made from limestone)	White or gray (often with black, red, or green stripes)	Hard and cold, can be grainy	Statues, buildings

21

Activities

Make a Rock Collection: Collect 10 rocks from around your neighborhood, house, and school. Try to find rocks of different colors, shapes, and sizes. Line them up on a table. Sort them into groups by color, then sort them by shape, then by how they feel. How many other ways can you group the rocks? Can you guess which rocks might be igneous, sedimentary, or metamorphic? To check your answers, find your rocks in a field guide to rocks and minerals.

Make Your Own Sandstone Brick: Mix $\frac{1}{2}$ cup (118 milliliters) water and $\frac{1}{2}$ cup (118 milliliters) white glue in a large cup or bowl. Fill a small milk carton with sand. Slowly add the glue mixture to the carton. Stop pouring when the mixture stops sinking into the sand.

Wait several days until the top of the sand has hardened and the box feels solid when you squeeze it. Peel the box away and admire your sandstone brick. It's soft like natural sandstone. You can scrape grains of sand off the brick with your fingernail.

Rock Solid Facts: Mohs Hardness Scale

Friedrich Mohs was a German scientist who lived in the 1800s. He came up with a way to help tell minerals apart.

The Mohs Hardness Scale lists 10 minerals, from the softest to the hardest. The softest mineral, talc, is number 1, and the hardest, diamond, is number 10.

HARDNESS	MINERAL
1	talc
2	gypsum
3	calcite
4	fluorite
5	apatite
6	orthoclase
7	quartz
8	topaz
9	corundum
10	diamond

Every mineral on this scale is able to scratch those with lower numbers. For example, calcite (3) scratches gypsum (2), but gypsum can't scratch calcite. A penny will scratch any of the minerals with a hardness of 3 or less. Try scratching a piece of classroom chalk firmly with a copper penny. What happens? What is the chalk's hardness?

Glossary

fossils—the hardened remains of dead plants or creatures found in some sedimentary rocks

gems—beautiful, rare minerals that have been crafted into jewelry

igneous (IG-nee-uhss) rock—rock that was once melted rock within the earth, then cooled and hardened

metamorphic (met-uh-MOR-fik) rock—rock that was changed from another kind of rock through heat and pressure

minerals—the materials that make up a rock. A rock may contain one, two, or many minerals.

sediment—a mixture of tiny bits of rock, shells, plants, sand, and minerals

sedimentary (sed-uh-MEN-tuh-ree) rock—rock that is made up of layers of sediment pressed together over thousands or millions of years

To Learn More

At the Library

Flanagan, Alice K. *Rocks.* Minneapolis: Compass Point Books, 2001.

Gallant, Roy A. *Rocks.* Tarrytown, N.Y.: Benchmark Books, 2001.

Gans, Roma. *Let's Go Rock Collecting.* New York: HarperCollins, 1997.

Hiscock, Bruce. *The Big Rock.* New York: Aladdin Paperbacks, 1999.

Hooper, Meredith. *The Pebble in My Pocket: A History of Our Earth.* New York: Viking, 1996.

Fact Hound

Fact Hound offers a safe, fun way to find Web sites related to this book. All of the sites on Fact Hound have been researched by our staff.

1. Go to *www.facthound.com*
2. Type in this special code: 1404800158
3. Click the FETCH IT button.

Your trusty Fact Hound will fetch the best sites for you!

Index